St. Paul's Church, Philadelphia

**The Commemoration**

of the fifty years of the Reverend Dr. John Andrews Harris as

minister-in-charge and rector

St. Paul's Church, Philadelphia

**The Commemoration**
*of the fifty years of the Reverend Dr. John Andrews Harris as minister-in-charge and rector*

ISBN/EAN: 9783337123154

Printed in Europe, USA, Canada, Australia, Japan

Cover: Foto ©Lupo / pixelio.de

More available books at **www.hansebooks.com**

## 1863-1913

—

# ST. PAUL'S CHURCH

## CHESTNUT HILL

### PHILADELPHIA

═══

The Commemoration of the Fifty Years of

THE REVEREND DR. JOHN ANDREWS HARRIS

AS MINISTER-IN-CHARGE AND RECTOR.

# TABLE OF CONTENTS.

# 1913

# SAINT PAUL'S CHURCH

## CHESTNUT HILL.

The fifty years of the services of the Reverend Dr. John Andrews Harris to his parish were commemorated on 15th and 16th June, 1913.

On 15th June, the fourth Sunday after Trinity, the Holy Communion was celebrated at two services as the highest possible expression of corporate and individual thanksgiving; and the sermon was preached by the Right Reverend, the Bishop of Pennsylvania. The Bishop was assisted in the services by the Reverend Dr. J. DeWolf Perry, Rector Emeritus of Calvary Church, Germantown, and President of the Standing Committee of the Diocese of Pennsylvania; the Reverend Dr. Samuel Upjohn, Rector of St. Luke's Church, Germantown; the Reverend Dr. John Andrews Harris, Rector of Saint Paul's, Chestnut Hill; the Reverend Dr. Thompson Cole, Rector of Saint Paul's Church, Cheltenham; the Reverend J. Clayton Mitchell, Rector of Calvary Church, Germantown, and formerly Curate of Saint Paul's, Chestnut Hill; and the Reverend J. Ogle Warfield, Curate of Saint Paul's, Chestnut Hill.

On the evening of 16th June, a meeting of the parishioners was held in the Church building, at which prayers were read by the Reverend J. Clayton Mitchell, hymns were sung by the choir and congregation, and addresses were made by C. Stuart Patterson, Esquire, Chairman of the meeting; by the Honorable William Potter, one of the Senior Vestrymen; by George Wharton Pepper, Esquire, and Francis A. Lewis, Esquire, Deputies of the Diocese of Pennsylvania to the General Convention of the Church, and by Edward S. Buckley, Jr., Esquire, the Rector's Warden. Mr. Buckley, on behalf of the parishioners and other friends of the Rector, presented to him a purse as an acknowledgement of the existence of a debt which the parish owed, and still owes to him, and which never can be paid.

There are printed in this record of the commemorative proceedings the sermon of the Right Reverend the Bishop of Pennsylvania, the speeches at the parish meeting, the Rector's sermon, and a list of the Rectors, Curates, Wardens, Vestrymen, pew-holders and seat-holders of the parish from its organization to the present time.

# SERMON

By

## The Right Reverend Philip M. Rhinelander,
### Bishop of the Diocese of Pennsylvania

15 June, 1913

✠

## "A GOOD SHEPHERD"

# A GOOD SHEPHERD.

"I am the Good Shepherd and I know mine own, and my own know me, even as the Father knoweth me, and I know the Father and I lay down my life for the sheep. And other sheep I have, which are not of this fold; them also I must bring and they shall hear my voice; and they shall become one flock and one shepherd."

*S. John* X: 14-17 (*R. V.*)

I suppose there is no word in human speech which so perfectly describes the relation of God to His people as the word "Shepherd." It is, of course, no substitute for the word "Father," but it does explain in terms of human need and human expectation, the meaning of God's Fatherhood. Sheep are very ignorant, and we, God's children, like sheep, are very ignorant, not knowing what is good or where is peace. Over against our ignorance stands God's sure and unswerving wisdom, Who knows us all and all things. Sheep are very weak and helpless, bound to destroy themselves, to surround themselves with perils, to become an easy prey to every enemy; and we, God's children, are very helpless before the storms of sin, and the onset of temptation, and the clouds and threatenings of sorrow. Over against our weakness stands the firm majesty of God's protection, always ready and always omnipotent to help. And finally, sheep are very wayward and very slow to learn, forgetting the simplest lessons, unreliable, untrustworthy; and so are we, forgetful, wilful, wayward. Over against our wilfulness and waywardness stands the unconquerable patience of God's love, who, loving, loves unto the end.

So, in pre-Christian ages, the vision of the Shepherd—God filled the prophet's eyes and stirred the Psalmists' hearts. If it were only true, if God were seen and known and realized as wisdom, strength and patience, available for each and all, then would all human needs be satisfied, all human faith fulfilled. So they sang and dreamed and praised and prayed. "The Lord is my shepherd; I shall not want. He maketh me to lie down in green pastures; he leadeth me beside the still waters." "He shall feed His flock like a shepherd; He shall gather the lambs with His arms and carry them in His bosom, and shall gently lead those that are with young." There is the great appealing vision, the great heartfelt aspiration. If only it were true, if only we could see and know it.

And behold, brethren, it is true and perfectly fulfilled

in Christ, who is Himself the answer to all human prayer, the revelation of God's perfect truth, the great 'Amen' of all God's promises; through Whom words become power, and revelation a blessed fact, and loving purposes a living Presence. So all that God had in heart and mind to give us, all that we and our forefathers were longing for, came actually to pass when the Eternal, Incarnate, Only Begotten Son of God, standing on this earth, among men and women such as we are, claimed and took the title, proclaimed to all men, and for all time, the truth: "I am the good Shepherd." That is the real meaning of the *goodness* of His Shepherding, namely, that it is no longer dream, but fact, no longer promise, but a great reality, that He is actually doing, or waiting to do, for each, for all, for always, the perfect work of shepherding. *For each, for all, for always;*—Christ in His individual devotion, the good Shepherd *for each,* because He knows each one and comes close up to him and stays close by him, and understands and watches each as though he were the only one. "I know Mine own, and Mine own know me." Christ, in His inclusive desire, the Good Shepherd, not only for each, but equally *for all.* As He walks up and down among His lambs and sheep, none the less His heart is always burning for those "other sheep" outside the fold as yet, whom He must bring and bless. "Other sheep I have," straying now upon the mountains as sheep not having shepherds: "Them also I must bring and they shall hear my voice; and they shall become one flock, one shepherd." Christ, in His unchanging faithfulness the Good Shepherd *for always.* The Life that He lays down is a life that has no end, that has passed through death that it might be forevermore available for each and every sheep. He, the good Shepherd, because He is the same yesterday, today and forever, can make good His word. "I am the good Shepherd."

Brethren, it belongs to Him, and Him alone, to speak that word and make that claim. But none the less, the Christian Ministry from the beginning has caught something of that vision and felt something of that responsibility. The under-shepherds are to be like the Perfect Shepherd. He will show through them some measure of His goodness. And our own Church, especially, has emphasized, and re-emphasized, this pastoral element of Ministry as its very heart and soul. Here lies the rule of the Church's Ministry and the test of all her Ministers. For this they are ordained and commissioned. For this they are given charge over the souls of men; that they may be good shepherds under Christ.

This ideal of shepherding has been exemplified in Him

for whose wonderful faithfulness and fruitfulness in ministry we are gathered here together this morning to render hearty and humble thanks to God. No other Priest in this whole Diocese; no other probably in the recollection of any of us here present; very few I think in the history of this Church from its beginning to the present time, have so brilliantly and beautifully reflected and reproduced before the eyes and hearts of two whole generations, the personal power and gracious goodness of the pastorate of Jesus Christ. The life of Doctor Harris has been a life of unrivaled richness of experience and of a great diversity of interests and activities. The Battle of Gettysburg had just been fought, and the news of it had just reached Philadelphia, on that very Sunday fifty years ago when he preached his first sermon as Minister in charge. Think of what the interval has meant in politics, in social life, in economic adjustments and reconstructions; in the building of cities and the movements of trade and population; in the expansion of the Gospel and the outflow of benevolence and social service; in the massed and massive strength of our Diocese; in the growth of our Institutions and in the unity and vigor of our life. In all and through all, his eyes have marked the signs, and his heart kindled with quick sympathies, and his mind analyzed with discerning judgment, and his will gone forth in strong, effective action and co-operation. In such a life, even such a crowded and thrilling history as that of the last half century finds both an accurate touchstone and a singularly comprehensive record. In such a life there are materials for volumes, for volumes bearing on, and dealing with, the chief causes and concerns of millions of our people in the most critical and searching period of their development.

And yet, summarizing the whole of it, separating the threads, grouping the incidents and interests, trying to say all very briefly, as we must, his life is above all else a compelling commentary on the work of the Good Shepherd. It is an inspired sermon preached, wrought out among us, that we may understand the meaning of the pastorate of Jesus Christ. "I am the good Shepherd and I know Mine own and My own know Me, and I lay down My life for My sheep; and other sheep I have which are not of this fold. Them also I must bring, and they shall become one flock, one Shepherd." The words and claims of Christ may fittingly and by His own blest will, be applied, as I have said, in their true degree of meaning to this, His faithful servant.

First, for his individual devotion to his flock. "I know my own and mine own know Me." How those words must thrill in the hearts of every member of this Parish! For fifty years this and this alone has been the rule of your Rector's life, and the dear desire of his heart. In sickness and in health, in youth and age, in joy and sorrow, in penitence and conflict, in doubts and fears, in prayers and praises, he has been knowing you, and calling you by name, and by that knowledge has been bringing the individualizing love of Christ Himself home as the very meaning of the Gospel, as the very hope of your salvation. And, on your side, you have been knowing him, and knowing him have been ready to follow where he has led and to prove your love, as love is always proved, by perfect trust. That is the supreme test of a good shepherd, the test set by Christ Himself. A stranger sheep will never follow, and how many shepherds are strangers to their sheep! Sheep do not follow, for they know not the voice of strangers. But the good shepherd calleth His own by name. That is the point. He knows each one by name, and so each follows Him, for daily food and drink, for health and healing; "out of the bondage of corruption into the liberty of the glory of the children of God." There is no more perfect, no more sacred bond than this. It is the holiest and most gracious of all earth's relationships. It is God's great gift to you.

And next, together with this individual devotion, has been a continual wise and earnest desire for the increase of the flock, for the enlarging of the fold, for the edification of the Church. "Other sheep I have which are not of this fold. Them also I must bring." I am not competent, either by depth of spiritual experience or by length of residence among you, to speak with authority of Dr. Harris' signal service to the Diocese and to the Church at large.

But I have at least seen and heard enough to make me quite confident that the position and prestige, which we as a Diocese have in the councils of the Church, and loyalty to our Mother, of which we rightly make our boast, and the unity which seems, thank God, Steadily to be gathering strength among us, are in chief measure due to his character, ability and influence. Devoted to his people and the Parish with a devotion which knows neither end nor limit, none the less there has been no element of parochialism in all his ministry. Breadth of vision, without a breach of party spirit, has marked all he has ever said or done. Absolute, unflinching loyalty to the Church's doctrine, discipline and worship, has been the unfailing record of his life. A kindling belief in the Church's mission and in the gracious plans and purposes which God would realize through

her in this new age and country, has been and is his ruling
motive and his constant aim. Love alone grows as it gives.
The more one loves, the more one finds it possible to love.
A shepherd's *goodness* consists finally in this, that, moving
about among his own loved sheep and lambs, calling, caring
for, feeding, healing, leading, guarding them, none the less
he is always conscious of, always praying for, always moved
with compassion over, the multitudes without, scattered
abroad, not having shepherds. These "other sheep" them
also, by all means and in all ways, "them also I must bring."
There is no peace, no end, no victory until all are won, until
there is one flock under One Shepherd.

So the story runs to its fulfillment. Individual devotion,
and inclusive desire both find their sum and crown in the record of an unchanging faithfulness. Brethren, the very es-
sence of the pastoral relation lies in its permanence. It is
a lifelong work. It is a life that must be laid down, and
given up; not a piece of it, but the whole of it; not one year,
or five years, or ten years, but, if God be gracious, fifty years
and more. For to know one single sheep means to know it
from its beginning to its ending. No mere cross section cut
ever yields the secret of a life. In all things that grow there
is "first the blade, then the ear, and then the full corn in the
ear." First the birth and baptism; then the teaching and the
confirmation; then the constant ministration of the Sacra-
ment of life; then the solemnity of Holy Matrimony and the
marvelous miracle of home and family; then the life work
and the full tide of life's responsibilities; then the waning
powers and the final weakness and the holy passing. To know
one single sheep means to know all this of one. Of course,
none knows us perfectly, save only Christ, the Living One,
the Eternal Shepherd and Bishop of all souls. But still, the
inner meaning of the ministry of the Good Shepherd does
come home to one, and I think no one else, who has followed
and has loved his own from the cradle to the grave. We are
so used to shifting, changing pastors, that we forget the
tragedy and loss involved when a flock is given over by one
shepherd to another. Of course it has to be. It is God's
ordering and the law of mortal life. Yet it is always and at
best, a mark of earthly imperfection. At worst, it is a griev-
ous treachery and the exposure of a hireling. But where,
and when, if God wills that there should be a life-long tend-
ing of the flock by one good shepherd, then there is a very
great and gracious revealing of His mercy. The fruits of it
are very evident. Strength, steadfastness, unity, a solid
sense of common interest, a deeply-rooted faith, high ideals

of duty, well established habits of religion, close knit and precious traditions of work and worship, a real Church home, a growing charity and household love, real intimations of immortality, bright glimpses of paradise and heaven, of the Church Expectant and the Church Triumphant—these are the ripe fruits of long continued pastoral relations, and these are yours.

Twenty-five years ago, your Rector spoke to you as follows: "There are conventional periods in the course of time when thought may be gathered together in a retrospect of the past in order to give a greater volume for its movement into the future, into the swellings of the great ocean of the unseen. The completion of a Rectorship in one Parish for a quarter of a century may not unnaturally be one of such periods. When two people have lived in peace together as man and wife that length of time, the 'silver wedding' marks an epoch in that joint life. The harmony of the past is an omen of hope, a pledge of stronger, deeper love for the future, even though the 'golden wedding' be a thing which the shortness and uncertainty of this mortal life forbids in most cases to anticipate." Those were his words, true in each detail except in that final prophecy that the "golden wedding" would not come. For here it is, bringing with it that stronger and deeper love of which twenty-five years ago there was so clear a promise.

For myself, I count it a personal privilege and pleasure beyond my power of expression, to be allowed to share in this celebration with you. I shall always remember it and treasure it. The life of the whole Diocese will be stronger for your strength and more joyful for your joy, more sweet and pure and holy for God's great goodness to you. May our Lord, who has so bountifully blessed and helped you here, carry you on to that still deeper and more lasting love and life where all fear is fled away and all sin and sorrow gone. May all this Parish, living and departed, young men and maidens, old men and children, priest and people, the shepherd and his flock, clear of all shadows, walking in the light, follow the Lamb forever, whithersoever He goeth, "lost in wonder, love and praise."

# THE MEETING OF THE PARISH ON THE EVENING OF MONDAY, 16TH JUNE, 1893.

---

C. STUART PATTERSON, ESQ., *took the chair.*

---

The Reverend, the Rector of Saint Martin's-in-the-Fields, brought to the meeting a letter which was read as an appropriate introduction to the proceedings:

June 16th, 1913.

THE REV. J. ANDREW HARRIS, D. D.
Rector, S. Paul's Church,
Chestnut Hill, Philadelphia.

Dear Dr. Harris:—

The Vestry of the Church of S. Martin-in-the-Fields convey to you their heartiest congratulations on the occasion of the celebration of the fiftieth anniversary of your connection with S. Paul's Church, Chestnut Hill, as Rector and Minister in charge. During the past twenty-four years the parish of S. Martin's has existed side by side with S. Paul's with unbroken relations of harmony and cordial friendship. This has been due to your own generous attitude at the beginning when S. Martin's was established within the parochial boundaries of S. Paul's; and to your unfailing courtesy and kindness in the years which followed. We wish to express our appreciation of your unselfish desire for the extension of the Church with your cordial sympathy toward the movement to found a new parish; and that both parishes have grown and prospered justifies the wisdom of your attitude where a less liberal policy would have resulted in a distinct loss to the Church at large.

Two parishes in such close proximity must necessarily feel each other's influence; and the example of the peace and harmony that has existed at S. Paul's has not been with-

13

out its fruit in the younger parish of S. Martin's. We wish not only to congratulate you on the culmination of these fifty years, crowned with the devoted love of your parishioners and the high respect of your neighbors, but we wish you many years of happiness in seeing the fruit of a long, wise and faithful ministry and in receiving the foretaste of its reward.

JACOB LEROY
Rector

SAMUEL FREDERICK HOUSTON
Rector's Warden

GEORGE WOODWARD, M. D.
Accounting Warden

NATHAN A. TAYLOR
L. ASHLEY FAUGHT, M. D.
HOLLINSHEAD W. TAYLOR
CHARLES E. VAN PELT
FRANCIS D. LEWIS
JOSEPH L. BRYAN
SAMUEL PORCHER
HENRY H. KINGSTON
Vestrymen

C. STUART PATTERSON, ESQ., said:

I have been asked to preside over this meeting to-night, because it was my good fortune to be present at some of the services and to hear some of the Rector's sermons in the early weeks of his incumbency in the summer of 1863; and also because Doctor Harris has honoured me with his friendship from a time long before either he, or I, had any expectation of living at Chestnut Hill.

Fifty years ago, Chestnut Hill was a country village with an individuality of its own. That day has long since passed. It is now only a part of a great metropolis. Rural lanes have been succeeded by city streets, and where there used to be broad meadows and ploughed fields, there are now rows of houses. With the growth of population, the membership of the parish has increased, and its activities have expanded to meet the changes of the times.

The conditions to-night are exceptional. For fifty years the pews have heard from the pulpit its words of warning, of counsel, and of affectionate entreaty. To-night, the pulpit is to hear from the pews their words of thanksgiving and of hope; of thanksgiving, that, for fifty years, the same voice has spoken to us from the altar and the pulpit, and of hope that that same voice may long continue to speak to us. It is, therefore, appropriate that he, whose every act and word for fifty years have been a blessing to his people, should to-night confine himself to the utterance of the words of benediction, which will conclude this meeting, and that he should, God willing, preach on Sunday next a sermon in which he can give us some of the impressions of his fifty years. He cannot, and, if he could, he would not, tell all of the story. No one could. He cannot tell us what effects his precepts and his example have had upon men he knows, and upon men he never has known. He cannot tell how efficacious those words and that example have been in keeping men to the straight and narrow path, and in preserving happiness to homes.

The strength of the bonds that bind the Rector to us, and that bind us to the Rector, is not only in that we have listened to his sermons for so many years, and in that we have reverently bowed before his ministrations at the altar. It is also in his daily life among us; in the happy marriages to whose wedding ceremonies he has brought the blessings of the Church; in the children whom he has held in his arms at their christening; the children, some of whom are now men and women of middle age, and some of whom are now in heaven; in the comfort he has brought in hours of sickness; and in the consolation he has given in days of sorrow.

The Rector preached his first sermon in this parish when the guns of Gettysburg and Vicksburg resounded through the land. Since then, there has been foreign war; there have been embittered political contests in the country; there has been dissension in the Diocese, and in the Church at large, but within these walls there always has been peace. Yet it never has been the peace of compromise, or of cowardice. The Rector has always had the courage of his opinions, and no man who cared to know could ever fail to know where he stood, and where he stands, upon every burning issue in Church or State. Within the parish, there have been wide variances of views upon the political and ecclesiastical questions of the day. There are such variances now. Nevertheless, there always have been, and, pray God, there always will be here, unanimity in devotion to the Church and in affection for the Rector, and mutual respect for honest differences of opinion.

That this has been, and is so, is largely because, for fifty years, the teaching from the pulpit has been that, so long as there is a world of sin, and misery, and wretchedness around us; so long as there are poverty to be relieved, suffering to be alleviated, and sorrow to be comforted; so long as men are to be saved from utter wreck and ruin; the Church has a work before it, which can best be done, if its people, bearing in mind their agreement in the essentials of the faith, and forgetting their minor and less important differences, do to the utmost of their abilities the duty of the hour.

It does not often happen amid the changes of this mortal life, that any human relation continues unbroken for fifty years. It does not often happen that a man of strong personality, a learned theologian, a preacher of convincing power, a pastor, "so anxious not to go to heaven alone," should steadfastly resist all allurements to wider and more attractive fields of duty, should resolutely put to one side every suggestion of ecclesiastical preferment, and should devote himself for half a century to the rectorship of one parish. All honour to Dr. Harris for so doing!

The Rector has always appealed to the intellects, as well as to the consciences, and to the affections, of his parishioners, and he has, in the past, and in the present, attracted to the service of the Church and to the work of the parish a singularly strong and earnest body of men and women.

"In these brave ranks I only see the gaps,
Thinking of dear ones whom the dumb turf wraps."

From these pews there rise before me memories of those who, in the past, have laboured for the church and who are not, in bodily presence with us to-night; gracious gentlewomen, who brought to the service of the Church their zeal, their devotion, and their boundless charity; fair maidens and stalwart youths, who knew only the springtime of life; soldiers, who never failed to heed the call of duty; grave merchants and captains of industry; skillful physicians; learned lawyers, some of them leaders of the bar; and, last, but not least, those who in their years of daily toil, kept the faith, and who are now enjoying in the realms of blessedness that peace and happiness, which were not given to them upon earth.

"What greetings come there from the voiceless dead,
What welcome, salutation, or reply,
What pressure from the hands that lifeless lie?
They are not here, they all are gone
Into the land of shadows—all save one.
Honour, and reverence, and the good repute
That follow faithful service as its fruit,
Be unto him, whom, living, we salute."

---

THE HONOURABLE WILLIAM POTTER said:

The history of the world is the biography of its great men. This has been truly said, and the character of a community is in the life of its representative men. This special community has, therefore, honored itself in honoring the rector of this Church, because it is a fact, that nothing shows the provincialism of a people so much, as when they forget to honor their representative men. The stranger coming to Saint Paul's often asks, why there are so many men in the congregation. Speaking as a man, and knowing the thoughts of other men, they come, because, in the materialistic struggle of the twentieth century, with the hardening environment of the six days' fight, they like to come to a service on the seventh, where they will not be given the stone of dogma and of creed controversy, but the bread of life. Many of you are familiar with that beautiful story in "Beside the Bonnie Brier Bush" of the good old Scotch widow with an only child, a son dedicated to the ministry. Overtaken with a fatal illness, she calls that son to her bedside and says: "The one great regret of my life is that I shall not be able to hear you preach your first sermon, but I shall be there in spirit, and I ask you, as a good soldier, to preach a sermon in the name of your great Captain, the Lord and Saviour, Jesus Christ;" and how, five years later, that young man coming back to preach in the village kirk, having prepared a sermon which he considers an unanswerable solution to all the controversies of the day, is reminded by his aunt of that dying prayer of his mother; and, taking that precious document to which he had devoted so much time, he throws it into the fire, and preaches a sermon upon the Lord and Saviour, Jesus Christ and the power of His resurrection, during the delivery of which, as the narrator states, you could almost feel that the Christ was in the kirk. It is such sermons that we secure from our rector, and it is not to be wondered at that men, hungering for spiritual food, come in large numbers to Saint Paul's.

We are celebrating the fiftieth year of a rector, who, before he ever became a rector, has always been a true man, and therefore has always preached from the standpoint of a man with his temptations, with his sorrows, and with his cares and tribulations. He has devoted himself to trying to teach us the mysteries of pain; the mysteries of sorrow, and the mysteries of death, and how, after all, they are swallowed up and are as nothing compared to the triumphant power of the Resurrection. It will be told you tonight by those competent to speak of the wonderful influence of this rector of ours, not only in the diocese of Pennsylvania, but in the Episcopal Church at large. I know of no man who is more devoted to its teaching, and yet I know of no man who is more catholic in the universality of his belief, that God's children are everywhere. Several years past, visiting Rome as a tourist, I met with a very dear friend who had just resigned his position of rector in the American College; and when I said to him, "Why have you resigned?" he said: "Because I was compelled to do so, for they consider I am too liberal in my views. We all take our creeds by the accident of birth, and no man or set of men, or church, can make me believe that all of God's people are in any one communion. I believe that every man, woman and child that tries to follow the example of the Master seven days in the week, and treats his fellow men as though they were his brethren, is not far from the Kingdom of God." The men, women and children that sit under the ministrations of this dear rector cannot help but feel that this incident typifies the character of preaching and consolation that we receive in St. Paul's.

If any one were to ask what is the chief characteristic

that makes Dr. Harris so beloved, so useful and so powerful in his influence, the answer from a close observer would come at once, "the pertinacity of his faithfulness to duty." Not the pertinacity of doggedness, but of constancy, steadfastness and real love of duty as the controlling influence of his life.

The American people in general and many of the St. Paul Parish in particular, are birds of passage and flit from place to place, as the seasons change. Who ever heard of Dr. Harris being away from Chestnut Hill? In the snows of January, or the heat of August, the poor or the rich, who need the sympathy of a loving rector, or the ministrations of his Church, can always find Dr. Harris, and it has been so for the half century of his faithful and devoted stewardship.

The rector's father was a graduate of the Military Academy at West Point. For ten years he served in the regular army, and then entered the Ministry. His son also attended a military school at West Point, (not the Military Academy) so that by ancestry, by education and by pre-disposition the rector has always been a good soldier in the army of his great Captain. He has helped more people than he has any conception of, to fight the good fight, in the midst of the weakness and sorrow of this mortal life. I know it is the sentiment of every man, woman and child in this congregation to-night, that our prayers shall go up without ceasing, that his lovely life may be spared for many years to come; for we feel of him that he is one of those of whom the Master said: "Be thou faithful unto death and I will give thee a crown of life."

---

GEORGE WHARTON PEPPER, ESQ., said:

If this were merely a parochial celebration I should feel that I had no place in the list of speakers. The honor in that event would be reserved for faithful vestrymen and those fortunate enough to be parishioners of Saint Paul's, such as Mr. Patterson himself and Mr. Potter and Mr. Buckley. I suppose that I might have been called upon as one of Doctor Harris's friends; and yet he has so many friends and admirers, and his relations to each are so intimate and personal, that any one of us would hesitate to attempt to represent the others. And if this occasion were merely a matter of diocesan interest, I should still be without excuse for speaking; because my friend, Mr. Lewis, who is to follow me, is much better qualified than I to speak of Doctor Harris's contributions to diocesan life. It is because this occasion is a matter of great moment to the church at large, because this anniversary is a matter of great public importance, that it may be permitted to a mere outsider to raise his voice here. And yet, in so speaking, I do not wish to ignore the personal tie which has bound me all my life to Doctor Harris. In my early childhood he was the companion in happiness of those who were near and dear to me, and when dark days came, he stood forth as the friend and the consoler. Indeed he is the first clergyman whom I distinctly recall, and Saint Paul's is the first church of which I have a vivid mental impression. In the long years that lie between, I have come to know, perhaps a thousand clergymen, but there are very, very few who can stand the test of comparison with him who in my consciousness first emerged as a representative of his order.

Any man whose active life has covered the last fifty years is one who has been called upon to face changes of vast import not only in the conditions of our external life, but in the characteristic tendencies of the world of thought within us. Nobody cares very much how laughable the efforts of the ordinary citizen may be when he attempts to adjust himself to these changes, but it is a matter of grave concern to us that our rector should be wise in his adjustment. If change finds him perverse and unsympathetic, he quickly loses his influence with the young. On the other hand, if he is quick to indorse every untried suggestion for social uplift and betterment, he soon loses the confidence of the mature. It seems to me a very fortunate circumstance that all his life Doctor Harris has been a teacher of youth. I know, for example, of his work at the Episcopal Academy, and I think I may venture the suggestion that he has never found himself in a more congenial environment than in the middle of a group of boys. The teaching experience has kept him young and has made him hospitable to new ideas; but on the other hand, he has been wise in insisting that change for the sake of change is not to be desired, and that the value of a hypothesis must be made clear before its acceptance is justifiable. He has always been a thinker, has Doctor Harris, but a conservative thinker; and that combination is so unusual that I venture to emphasize it. I have known a great many men whose conservatism has been wholly untouched by thought, and a great many thinkers whose conclusions have never been restrained by reverence. There has been nothing parochial or narrow or provincial in the scope of Doctor Harris's interests. He has always been keenly alive to community problems, and he has stood forth as the courageous champion of righteousness in civic life and he has been in touch with the whole circle of church work and life beyond the limits of the parish and the diocese. His service in the General Convention, though brief, was useful, and it is to be regretted that he would not permit himself to serve longer as a deputy; for the church always stands in need of men in her councils who combine, as he does, practical wisdom and vital Christianity.

In the early part of the fifty years of his service here, the tendency among Christian people to disintegrate in their church relationships had not yet been checked. Within the limits of that fifty-year period new sects and novel cults have come into existence. Perhaps we fail to realize it, but the fact is that there are many large and influential groups of Christians aspiring to be known by the noble name of "churches" whose lives are shorter, not merely than the life of this parish, but shorter than the period of Doctor Harris's ministry. Under such conditions there sometimes arises in a man's breast the suspicion that after all there are no fundamental and fixed beliefs, and that Christianity is merely a generic term for various individual apprehensions of truth. I call upon such a man to reassure himself by contemplating the continuous witness which our church has borne, not merely to the validity, but to the intellectual necessity of fixed beliefs. I remind him that we place our emphasis upon holy orders, not because an order involving the idea of succession is merely a governmental scheme, but an institution for the conservation of fixed and fundamental ideas. We should be devoutly thankful that such an order is our Catholic heritage, and profoundly grateful, too, that we are continually refreshed and revived by insistence on the principle emphasized so strongly in the Reformation, that all organization must be vitalized by devotion, and that God is Spirit, and that those who worship Him must worship Him in spirit and in truth. It was into an order so conceived that, called by the Spirit, Doctor Harris stepped early in the days of his service, and from that time onward his life and work became the manifestation of that continuity for which his order stands. His has been the clear vision which enables him to see that fixed and fundamental Christian truths are few and simple. Not the least important part of his message has been his insistence to his parishioners that the controversies of history have raged rather about the man-made explanations of divine facts than about the facts themselves. It is as if he had been insistent in reminding us of the difference between astronomy and the stars. The men of science may differ as they will respecting their theories of the universe, but all the while the stars keep on shining.

My friends, an occasion such as this must have in it an element of pain to Doctor Harris, for, if I know him, and I think I do, while we are eulogizing him, there must be uppermost in his mind the thought of his own unworthiness. I am sure that if he were to speak to-night, he would tell you that far more valuable to him than words of eulogy, would be a spiritual fruitage of his ministry, manifested in the devoted lives of his parishioners. If the time past in his life has sufficed for the seed-time it is for us, his parishioners and friends, to see to it that the remaining years of his ministry are the years of harvest—the time for the garnering of the grain. If we let this fiftieth anniversary go by without renewing our pledges of loyalty to Our Lord, without forming afresh our own resolutions of noble living, he may well lament the comparison between the petty done and the undone vast. Memory, my friends, is a mere luxury unless from its storehouse we can draw inspiration for the work of the future. We should be eager to recall the events of this long ministry chiefly because they are a challenge to us to act in the living present. I know that I do not misinterpret the thought in Doctor Harris's heart to-night if I conclude with the suggestion that, after all words of eulogy have been said, we shall bring greater gladness into his heart than in any other way if we unite in praying from the bottom of our hearts the fervent prayer of the poet:

"Lord God of Hosts, be with us yet,
Lest we forget—lest we forget."

FRANCIS A. LEWIS, ESQ., said:

I do not recall, Mr. Chairman, ever to have received an invitation which gave me greater personal pleasure to accept than that which brings me here to-night, and this for two reasons. First, it is a privilege to do honor to the Rector of this Church, a Rector of such long standing, and secondly, there is a personal pleasure involved, because my boyhood and early manhood were spent in this parish. It is a sort of privilege to be brought back to what may be called a family gathering. If in what I shall very briefly say I may seem to dwell more upon the past than upon the present, it is not with any intention to disparage what may have happened in the last twenty-five years, but simply because my knowledge of the parish was that of the earlier time.

What was Chestnut Hill when Doctor Harris came here in 1863? It was simply the summer residence of a number of well-to-do people of Philadelphia. It was crude, yes, very crude. It was inconvenient, exceedingly inconvenient. Trains ran only on one road, and these at two hours' interval, and their going or prospective going was always signalized by the blowing of a five-minute whistle. Those were the days when Doctor Harris came here, and similar conditions obtained for years thereafter. But was that all of it? Oh, no. He came to minister to a very remarkable congregation, a congregation of which I do not know where to find the exact counterpart. I have no objection to mentioning names. These men are all dead and gone, but their memory lives, and I shall mention them because in the retrospect that I make here of my boyhood and young manhood, I can see them sitting in these very pews. I can see Alexander Biddle and John Bohlen, Judge Thayer and Richard Vaux, William Henry Trotter and Richard C. McMurtrie, Charles Platt and Edward S. Buckley, Caleb Cope and George W. Biddle and George C. Morris, and many more whom I cannot recall just at the moment, but whom I do not mean to neglect. They represented everything that was good, everything that was intelligent, everything that was astute, everything that stood for good in the community in which they lived. What must have been the influence of a Rector such as Doctor Harris upon those men, and what must have been the influence of those men upon Doctor Harris? It is only necessary to suggest such a thing to have you follow out your own line of thought to a conclusion. Living in a summer community, although constantly enlarging, having in front of him every Sunday and to talk to every week day, men of this calibre, must have been an inspiration to him; and he came with a trained mind to his work, not only with a trained mind but with a good spirit, to pass his lot in amongst these people, and to have what is called his influence over them. There is a great mistake as to what influence is. Influence must be preceded by effluence. A man who is to be influenced must be influenced because something has flown into him out of somebody else, and that is exactly what happened both from Doctor Harris on his people, and from his people upon him. Then again, some men are always courting influence, some men are always trying to see how influential they can be. But someone has said: "Influence is like originality, the way to get it is to forget it." The man who tries to be influential may become powerful as some very rich man because of his money, but one will never become influential unless his force of character, his force of goodness, his force of standing for something creates the influence from him.

I recall many of those early days very well. I recall the night of Lee's surrender, when my own dear father called on Doctor Harris in the middle of the night, or Doctor Harris called on him, I do not remember which, and they went down on that April night to ring that bell there to tell of the victory of Grant over Lee. It was in a pew over yonder that I heard in a whisper from my father the Saturday before the Easter, 1865, of the assassination of Mr. Lincoln. There is one other thing that has always impressed me, and that was the way in which Doctor Harris so particularly understood and so well realized how to deal sanely with people's idiosyncrasies, if you so choose to call them. For example, I distinctly recall that the length of the sermon was always in summer time when I lived here in the inverse ratio to the height of the thermometer. If you came here on a cool Sunday you might get a twenty-five minute sermon, but if you came with the thermometer at 90, there was not the smallest probability of it. The spirit may have been willing, but the weakness of the congregational flesh was realized. The sermons made impressions on those who heard them. They made impressions upon my boyish mind. I suppose our beloved church has a reason for everything it does. I do not know what the particular reason is that the story of Joseph and his various vicissitudes should be assigned to the warmest Sunday mornings in summer, but so they are. It may be because Joseph was something of a dreamer and heat invites sleep and dreams. It may be because he passed a large portion of his life in Egypt, which has a very hot climate; but whatever the reason, we always hear the story of Joseph read over again in the summer. Doctor Harris was quite equal to this, and I recollect a sermon that he prepared in the early years of his ministry from the text, "Behold this dreamer cometh." It was a wonderful sermon, it was a lurid sermon; and as it was preached at least bi-ennially I became thoroughly familiar with its contents. But there was always a demand for that sermon.

Now one who can preach sermons which leave an impression on the mind forty years afterwards, not only of their text but of their contents, must be having a very large spiritual influence on the community to which he preaches, and that is evidenced by the large number of people who are constantly attending this church. His church was always full in summer time, in winter not so full because there were not so many people here. And it was not a cool church. I recollect that one of the issues of the early times here in this church, was the question, what point the thermometer had to reach in order that yonder door should be kept open. Mr. Caleb Cope sat where I see my friend Mr. Samuel Dickson now sitting, and he was a very old man. He sang, sometimes at variance with the choir, but he always sang; and that door was never under any circumstances to be opened on his head, because it created a draft likely to give him cold. Those were some of the incidents of Doctor Harris's early ministry, albeit perhaps not important, yet making some impression on a childish mind.

I have been asked to say a word, and I very gladly do so as to Doctor Harris's influence in the diocese of Pennsylvania. He came into the ministry under the greatest bishop that the diocese of Pennsylvania has ever seen, Alonzo Potter; and no one with any mind could come into the ministry under his directorship, so to speak, without in a measure imbibing some of the good sense, the sound judgment, the profound wisdom if you choose to call it, of that great man. In all these years he has sat in the Convention, and I have happened to have been with him there for thirty years past. If I am asked to point out the distinguishing characteristic of Doctor Harris's influence upon the diocese of Pennsylvania, I should call it his sanity, his looking at things from a sane point of view. There are so many people who mean well and are perfectly justified in remaining outside an insane asylum, but nevertheless have not what are called sane minds. He always looked at what practically could be done to produce a given result. If he saw visions he kept them to himself, the man is wise who does, because people who see visions are very apt to be visionary. So it is, that through these years his influence has always been extending, always been widening, always been broadening, simply because, with the ripeness

of his years has come the grand sanity of his judgment.
Mr. Pepper alluded to the fact that he had sat in a General
Convention. If the Diocese of Pennsylvania has had its
way, he would be sitting there still, and it is a great pity
that he refused to continue a Deputy long years ago, because, as he once confided to me, he regarded the General
Convention as a great bore. It probably is, but at the same
time some of us have got to go there, and I always regretted
very much that a man like Doctor Harris had not been
willing to sit there all these years and contribute his sanity
and ripe judgment to so many of the problems that come
before that body.

I must not go on. The time allotted to me has already
I should imagine more than expired. But as I stand here
in this church to-night, my mind is filled not only with the
memories of which I have spoken, but with a profound
thankfulness to Almighty God that this particular function,
the particular meetings of yesterday and to-day, have actually taken place; and I have reason for saying this. The
incident may not be unfamiliar to you all, it may possibly
be known to some. A number of years ago there died in
New York one of the most remarkable men that our church
has ever produced, the Reverend Edward Washburn, at the
time of his death Rector of Calvary Church, New York.
After the funeral services had been held, the clergy who
were present asked permission to meet in the late Rector's
study, that they might pass some appropriate resolutions
upon his death. Permission was granted, and the meeting
was in progress. Speech after speech had been made by
the clergy present, dwelling as they well might, in the highest terms on his wonderful mind, his wonderful character,
his wonderful genius, his wonderful ability; and as they
were pouring out these true but belated words, the door
of the study, which no one noticed to have been ajar, was
suddenly thrown open and into this meeting came a woman,
the widow of Doctor Washburn, her hands held together,
tense with grief, tense with excitement; and she said to
those men, "Oh, gentlemen, if you loved Edward so much,
why did you not tell him so when he was alive?" Doctor
Harris, it is because we all love you so, that we have come
here to tell you so when you are alive.

EDWARD S. BUCKLEY, JR., ESQ., said:

I am very sure that I can add but little to what has been so well said here to-night, but I have been given a very great privilege, and I feel that the only claim that I have to the great pleasure before me, lies in the fact of my long connection with Saint Paul's Parish, that it has been my privilege to have been one of your flock, my dear sir, throughout your whole incumbency, and that ever since I was a very little child, you have been to me a father. As I stand here to-night and look back over the past fifty years, I cannot help but feel that I am here to speak not only for those whose privilege it is to be with you now, but for all those to whom you have so faithfully ministered and whom we believe, under your guidance, are now numbered among the saints of God at rest. It would be easy to give figures to show the wonderful work which you have accomplished at Chestnut Hill, but figures cannot tell the whole or even the best part of what you have done for the people of Saint Paul's. You have taken many of us in your arms and placed the Master's own sign upon our brows. You have taught us and led us to the Bishop to receive the gift of the Holy Ghost, and with your own hands you have given to many of us our first communion. You have blessed and sanctified in God's name our marriages, you have ministered to our sick and dying, you have laid to rest those whom we have loved and who now stand in His presence, and testify that through long years, by day and by night, always faithfully, always lovingly, you have fed His sheep, you have fed His lambs. I believe that in a very real sense they are with us to-night, and in their name and in the name of this congregation, your flock there and your flock here, I beg you to accept this gift as an evidence of the love of all those for whom your life has been spent.

---

Mr. Buckley then handed to the Rector a pocketbook containing a certificate of deposit for a sum of money which had been contributed by the parishioners, and by other friends of the Rector, as an expression of their respect and affection for him.

The Rector then pronounced the benediction and the meeting adjourned.

# SERMON

OF THE

## REVEREND JOHN ANDREWS HARRIS, D. D.

DELIVERED AT

## ST. PAUL'S CHURCH
### CHESTNUT HILL

ON

22d JUNE, 1913

AT THE REQUEST OF THE VESTRY

# AN HISTORICAL SKETCH OF ST. PAUL'S PARISH

About the middle of the last century there was apparently no probability that such a parish as St. Paul's now is would ever be here. What led to its formation is thus stated by its first rector in the parish register:

The beginning of Episcopal services at Chestnut Hill was, as far as can be ascertained, in the early fifties of the last century. Mrs. Anna M. Scheetz, then residing on the Hill, having been educated in the Protestant Episcopal Church, was desirous to secure for herself and neighborhood the benefit . . . of its calm order and elevated Christian influence, and by special effort secured, for a short time, the ministrations of the Rev. George Hopkins, then residing in Philadelphia, without parochial charge. The material for a congregation then, however, was too scanty. Very few Episcopalians were to be found throughout the neighborhood. Other denominations of Christians had almost a monopoly of the ground. Strong prejudices existed in the minds of many against the church. After a somewhat languishing life of but a few months, the removal of Mrs. Scheetz to Philadelphia put an end to the effort for a time.

The population of the Hill meanwhile went on increasing. The beauty of the surrounding scenery, the elevation and healthfulness of the position, the nearness to the city of Philadelphia, and the gradual growth of the facilities of communication with it, made the place more and more one of desirable resort, especially for summer residence. The artistic taste of Colonel Cephas G. Childs, then a resident in Germantown, was strongly attracted by the beauties of the region. He visited it frequently in his daily drives; became more and more interested in it; drew the attention of his numerous friends to it, and, finally, made it his place of residence, in 1852 or 1853. To him and his efforts the growth of the place from that time is very greatly due. His large acquaintance, his well-known taste, and the enthusiasm with which he threw himself into any favorite enterprise, contributing to bring the Hill more and more into notice, and induced an increasing desire with many to avail themselves of its advantages. Among those who early

31

secured these for themselves by the purchase of lots and erection of residences were William Platt, Esq., with his sons, Clayton T., Charles and William, his daughter, Mrs. Emily Pepper, widow of David Pepper, Esq., and his son-in-law, Dr. William Pepper; John Bohlen, Esq., with his mother, Mrs. Jane Bohlen, and sister Miss Catharine; Thomas Earp, Jr., Esq.; Charles Taylor, Esq.; William Henry Trotter, Esq.; John C. Bullitt, Esq., and Mrs. Alicia Price, with her sisters, Miss Sophia Sweeney and Anna Sweeney. These all had been either trained in the Protestant Episcopal Church or from connections and associations were more or less attached to it. The same was the case with Frederic Fairthorne, Esq., who (though later) resided for some time on the Hill in a house belonging to Thomas Earp, and who subsequently purchased for himself a place in Roxborough, three miles away.

Some of the above named—as Colonel Childs and Mr. Earp—worshiped for a time with the Presbyterians for want of any service of their own church. Others—as Mr. Bohlen and the Platt family—attended services at St. Thomas' Church, Whitemarsh. But the inconvenience of such attendance operated with the increase of population, and the prospect of further increase from the opening of the railroad to Philadelphia to excite the desire for church services upon the Hill. Accordingly, on the 4th of July, 1853, in a private interview in the house of Mr. John Bohlen, it was resolved between himself, Colonel Childs and Mr. Charles Platt to institute Episcopal worship for at least the remainder of that summer. These gentlemen, with Mr. Charles Taylor and Mr. Earp, undertaking to meet the expense of such services as should be instituted. The little Union Chapel, on Sheridan Lane, the birth place of most of the churches on the Hill, was the place selected for the commencement of the enterprise, and on the second Sunday in July the Rev. Kingston Goddard, then rector of the Church of the Atonement, Philadelphia, held there the opening service for the little company of Episcopalians on the Hill. Subsequently, the same gentleman more than once kindly officiated, as did Dr. Newton, of St. Paul's, Philadelphia; the Rev. Dudley A. Tyng, of the Church of the Epiphany; the Rev. Charles D. Cooper, of St. Philip's; the Rev. Charles H. Wheeler, of the Episcopal Female Institute, Philadelphia; the Rev. Mr. Lonnsbery, of St. Jude's; the Rev. Mr. Woods, the Rev. Mr. Atkins, and others. As may be supposed from the length of the list of clergymen, the services did not close with the summer, according to the first design. They were found to be so pleasant, awakened so much interest and secured such an attendance from persons not specially connected with the church that even when the summer residents returned to the city they were continued mainly under the direction and through the active exertions of Colonel Childs throughout the ensuing winter and spring.

On the return of the summer a meeting was called for the regular organization of a Protestant Episcopal congregation, and in pursuance of such a call there assembled in the large hall of the railroad depot, June 18, 1855, Colonel and Mrs. Childs, Mr. John Bohlen, Mr. Clayton T. Platt, Mr. and Mrs. Charles Platt, Mr. and Mrs. Earp, Mr. and Mrs. Fairthorne, Mr. Houston, Mrs. Thomas Mason, Mr. and Mrs. Jerram, Mrs. David Pepper, Mrs. Price, Miss Sophia Sweeney, Miss Steinbenner, Miss M. W. Fobes. Colonel C. G. Childs was called to the chair and Thomas Earp, Jr., appointed Secretary.

A preamble and resolutions affirming the necessity for the formation of an Episcopal congregation on the Hill were offered by John Bohlen, Esq., seconded by Charles Platt, Esq., and adopted without a dissenting voice. After an address from Mr. Bohlen, stating the objects proposed to be accomplished, declaring the importance of the movement entered on, and urging that it be prosecuted seriously and with prayer, those present proceeded to elect eleven vestrymen, and with entire unanimity the following named gentlemen were chosen: John Bohlen, Cephas G. Childs, Charles Platt, Joseph H. Hildeburn, Charles Taylor, Thomas Earp, Jr.; Frederic Fairthorne, Clayton T. Platt, John C. Bullitt, William Henry Trotter and Thomas Mason.

The organization of the Parish—which it was resolved should be called St. Paul's Church, Chestnut Hill—being thus effected, the establishment of a Sunday-school was at once decided on. On motion of Mr. Charles Platt a meeting was called for this purpose on Thursday evening, June 21st, and on that evening the preliminary arrangements for a Sunday-school were made. John Bohlen, Esq., and Colonel Cephas G. Childs were constituted Superintendents—the former to act from June to November, the latter for the remainder of the year. Mrs. Childs, Mrs. Price and Miss Sweeney were, with these gentlemen, especially active in the gathering of the Sunday-school and rendered efficient service in it when it was formed. . . .

Mr. Mason and his wife, Mrs. Jerram and a young man named John Johnson, also assisted in the school during its first year. The number of pupils from the first was small, nearly all the children on the Hill having been gathered into other Sunday-schools before this was organized; but there were some interesting elements and an excellent feeling in the school.

On the 25th day of June the vestry was fully organized by the election of Colonel Childs as Rector's Warden, Frederic Fairthorne as Accounting Warden and Thomas Earp, Jr., as Secretary. Mr. Bohlen and Mr. Charles Platt were charged with the duty of preparing a charter. With thanks to the Trustees of the Union Chapel for its use during the past year, it was determined to hold the services, now established in the hall of the railroad depot as being at once more central, more spacious and more pleasant.

The Rev. R. W. Oliver had been engaged as minister for the parish for several months, served faithfully till the beginning of November, and then retired to enter on Missionary work in the Western portion of the Diocese.

On November 6th the Minutes of the Vestry stated that the Rev. Alexander Shiras, who had been two months before informally invited to the rectorship, was unanimously elected rector. He entered on his duties November 16, 1855.

---

So much, then, for the story of the founding of the parish and the men and women who took part from the beginning of the movement till its accomplishment, and in some of the stages of its progress, but who have now entered into rest.

Before recording the succeeding steps of the parochial history, it is well to recall the names of others, both women and men, also now "gone before," who have aided and established the growth of the parish and its influence in this neighborhood and in the diocese of Pennsylvania.

Among the women who influenced for good both the social life and the ecclesiastical usefulness of St. Paul's, or who took a deep interest in its work, may be cited, besides those above mentioned in the story of the founding of the parish: Mrs. Matthew Brooke Buckley, Mrs. Edmund Watmough and her daughters, Mrs. M. Russell Thayer and Miss Juliana Watmough, Mrs. St. George Tucker Campbell, Mrs. Clayton T. Platt, Miss Ellen R. Brown, Mrs. Richard Norris, Mrs. Frank W. Ralston, Mrs. Henry Reed, Mrs. Joseph P. Smith, Mrs. John Welsh, Jr., Mrs. George C. Morris, Mrs. William B. Reed, Mrs. Richard H. Rush, Mrs. Edward H.

Trotter, Mrs. William H. Trotter, Mrs. Charles Taylor, Mrs. J. Lowber Welsh and Mrs. Joseph Patterson, all these have been gathered into the fold, as yet unseen by mortal eyes, where the veil is withdrawn and they see the Good Shepherd face to face. The influence they exercised while living in the parish still lives and has put its stamp upon the *tone* of it. And as for the men (still omitting the repetition of names already mentioned as among the founders of the parish) who have given tone to it and in their several walks in life have exercised a weighty influence in the community in which they lived or in the wider sphere of national matters, civil and military, on land or sea, we recall among those who by the Master of the feast have been "called from labor to refreshment," such as Messrs. Russell Thayer, Edward S. Buckley, Benoni Lockwood, Richard C. McMurtrie, Richard Norris, John C. Sims, Jr.; William C. Mackie, John P. Brock, Henry Wharton, Alexander Biddle, Joseph W. Baker, John Whittaker, Richard C. Dale, William C. Atwood, Edwin N. Benson, James C. Biddle, Dr. Robert Bolling, St. George Tucker Campbell, Caleb Cope, Alfred M. Collins, Frederic Collins, Edmund P. Dwight, William E. Goodman, Samuel Goodman, Jr., A. Groves, Jr.; George Harding, William W. Harding, General Herman L. Haupt, Charles Heebner, Morton P. Henry, Samuel S. Hollingsworth, R. Winder Johnson, Prof. Francis A. Jackson, Spencer M. Janney, Lawrence Lewis, Francis A. Lewis, Sr.; Robert M. Lewis, Henry S. Lowber, John T. Montgomery, George C. Morris, Henry L. Norris, Joseph Patterson, David Pepper, Dr. George Pepper, J. Sergeant Price, Francis W. Ralston, William B. Reed, Thomas Robins, Benjamin Rush, Moncure Robinson, Colonel Richard H. Rush, Furman Sheppard, Samuel L. Shober, Theodore Starr, Isaac Starr, Sr.; Edward H. Trotter, George C. Thomas, Edward H. Trotter, Louis C. Vanuxem, Richard Vaux, Tobias Wagner, Pendleton G. Watwough, John Welsh, Jr.; Henry Wharton, John Whittaker, John Lowber Welsh and John Zebley.

From the list of those who have been prominently instrumental in one way or another in building up the parish of St. Paul's, we may revert to the history of its progress, from the first rectorship, that of the Rev. Alexander Shiras, beginning in 1855. He resigned in 1860. To fill the vacancy, the Rev. William H. Hare was elected and entered on his duties on March 19, 1861. By this time Chestnut Hill had begun to attract many more people as a place of residence, for many only a summer residence, owing to the poor traveling facilities given by the railroad of those days, and the small congregation soon outgrew the chapel. The cornerstone of the new church, the one in which we now are, was laid by Bishop Alonzo Potter, on October 25, 1861. The church was opened for divine service on June 15, 1862, with every prospect of growing with the population, but, unfortunately, the illness of Mrs. Hare necessitated a change of climate by the physician's orders, and Mr. Hare was granted a six months' leave of absence, the vestry asking a friend of his to administer the parish during his absence, beginning with July 5, 1863; and that day coming up here from Germantown, where I lived, will never be forgotten. Nobody knew where the Army of the Potomac was. There were all sorts of rumors, and as I came from the house I lived in in Germantown to the railroad station there was something in the air. You know what an awful hush there is sometimes before a blasting thunder storm—everything quiet, even the birds cease twittering. There was just that sort of fog hanging over everything here. "What next?" people were saying, and as I came along, walking part way along the railway from Germantown to the main street where the depot then was, there were groups of men standing along the railroad talking. They were not talking in voices louder than that I am using just now, you could not hear what was said, but there they were waiting—waiting, some of them trembling, and it was through an atmosphere of this sort that I came here for my first service, under the arrangement with the vestry to relieve Mr. Hare.

The rector's warden very courteously asked me to dine with him, and on our way back to the service that afternoon we met a prominent man of Philadelphia who was living here, who had a private telegram—Gettysburg was won! Lee was in retreat! People do not forget those days very easily. It was not known in the city until the night services of the churches, and when I went home in the afternoon I met similar groups of men standing just where I had seen them in the morning, talking, whispering, not knowing anything about it. It got abroad in the city I believe about 9 o'clock, the time of the night services there, and there were Te Deums galore all through.

The same cause—to go back to the story—which necessitated Mr. Hare's going away prevented his return, unfortunately, and his substitute was chosen to succeed him in January, 1864, thus as minister in charge and rector, serving for fifty years—and a pleasanter service no rector has ever had. Thank God and thank you!

Of course, coming in this way, it was my duty and my

pleasure to keep things exactly, so far as I could, as Mr. Hare had left them. His involuntary, but necessary, resignation of the rectorship, while it was a blow to this parish, was fortunately ordered by Divine Providence to be a great blessing to the church at large. No Bishop in this church has left a more magnificent record of his devoted work than did he who became the Right Reverend William Hobart Hare, Doctor of Divinity. When he left this parish, soon afterwards he was appointed secretary of the Committee of the General Board of Missions, of Foreign Missions, and that brought him into prominence in the Church, and he had so ministered his office in that capacity that when it was a question in the General Convention of sending out somebody to the Far West to minister to the souls of the wild Indians there, he was chosen. He was assigned the district called the Missionary District of Niobrara, in South Dakota, which was inhabited chiefly by Indians, and the magnificent work he did there, the perils he went through, the labors he performed, the devotion that he showed, cannot be properly expressed in words. Afterwards he became Bishop of South Dakota, which was an enlarged sphere, including both whites and Indians of Niobrara. The part of his life work as completed in succeeding years was one of weariness and painfulness. He suffered intense pain all the time, but never faltered. He, if any man could become such, was a Christian hero, and if he had not been removed from this parish, owing to the causes mentioned, and his being translated to the broader sphere of the Board of Missions, he might never have been so well known. So, when I came here as I say, owing to these causes, I wanted to keep things just as he left them. It was my pleasure and my duty to do it. I found, soon after coming, in what is now Springfield Avenue, then called Wissahickon Avenue, which was near St. Martin's Church of the present day, that prayer meeting and Bible class combined had been formed, and two or three of the earnest laymen of the parish used to go down on Sunday nights and gather the people together in one another's house, one after the other, and singing and praying and teaching them. Most of them were mill hands at that time. Those mills on Cresheim Creek, just below the Institution for Deaf and Dumb, were in full operation, and employed a great many hands. There were some others who lived in the neighborhood of about the same station in life who came to these classes. They met, as I say, at each other's houses, but the devil came sometimes with them; because there got to be exhibitions of petty jealousy and fault-finding and all that sort of thing, and so it seemed better to build a small mission chapel just at that place, where everybody would stand on common ground. St. Paul's congregation very kindly and promptly agreed to do it, bought a lot at quite a reasonable price and constructed a small plain chapel there, which I think would hold 120 people. There was a Sunday-school conducted in it in the afternoon by a devoted woman in the parish here, Miss Ellen R. Brown, and at night, every Sunday night, for two or three years, I went down there to hold a regular service. As long as the mills kept open it was pretty well filled; but the mills closed after a while, and a great many of those who came there to worship through the instrumentality of the teachings I speak of, had become confirmed in the church, and its usefulness as a mission field ceased. It was disposed of at quite a good price and the money used for other church purposes. But that mission did a great deal of good. It was Mr. Hare's work in starting it, and it turned out, I fancy, to exceed his expectation in the results.

The debt upon the church building was paid and the church consecrated on October 16, 1865, during the session of the General Convention of a reunited Church in that year. I came here, as I said, amid the clash of arms. The church was consecrated at the time of a reunited church that had been severed by the sword, and surely it was an omen of peace for the parish. There were clergymen here from North and South, and that made it into a full-grown church, consecrated 1865. The rectory was finished in November, 1868. The interior of the church is not what it was at first. At first it was very bare and barn-like, rather depressing. Some changes were made in the winter of 1867, both in the chancel and the ceiling of the church, which made some improvement. In 1882, by a voluntary gift of Mr. Edwin N. Benson, the present chancel was built and a stained glass window—"Christ blessing little children"—was inserted. Then, by testamentary gift from the late Mrs. Tobias Wagner, the erection of a parish building was made possible, and it was finished in 1889. Before that we had no place of meeting for any church society except in the Sunday-school building, and that was rather chilly for any sociable meeting. Consequently the work somewhat flagged. It was never crowded, by the way, and so this parish building was found to be—it was thought it would be, and it has proven the correctness of the thought—a very great help in parish work. It is used for everything in connection with weekday work of the parish, and on Sunday it is used as you know, for infant schools and Bible classes and the choir.

The memorial baptistry was built in 1902. The Accounting Warden of this Church, Mr. Alexander C. Humphreys, was compelled by business exigencies to move away to New York, and was very much missed. His eldest son was married, and he, with his bride and younger brother, went to Egypt and up the Nile. By some accident, nobody knows how or what the accident was, the younger brother, a lad of about twelve, fell overboard. His brother immediately plunged after him, and they never saw them alive again. That baptistry records the tragic event.

Another matter in connection with the history of the church is the endowment fund that was inaugurated in 1904. By annual accretions it now amounts to nearly $18,000. At the end of the next fifty years, at its present rate of growth, it may reach a figure which will be of important value to the parish. Nothing can be taken from it or used in any way, except to accumulate interest, until it reaches the sum of $50,000.

I want to speak of another thing, and that is the value of lay co-operation in this parish. Of course it is so in every parish, but in this parish it has been growing, growing steadily; and going down even to such small matters, looked at in one way, as the giving of a cup of cold water to some of Christ's needy ones, which will not lose its reward. Its growth and earnestness is a very large element in the prosperity of this parish. I wish to emphasize this fact, that the whole-hearted devotion of the members of this congregation in this good work they are doing, in the good work they are upholding outside of the parish as well as in, has done far more to build this parish up to its present status than anything the rector has ever done. I want that clearly understood. One of the things that have come about by the lay co-operation, speaking first of something which is an act of the laity, is the choir of the church. If you had been here on the 5th of July, 1863, you would have heard no such help to the worship of Almighty God as you now hear. The choir at that time was a voluntary one, a very small one. The instrument, which was called a seraphine, certainly did not emit heavenly music, neither did it put forth good earthly music. But that was the beginning of the thing. It required work, manly and womanly, because it was a mixed choir; and after we got a new organ there it still continued in its place, and was a mixed choir. Then a time came, by, I believe, the almost universal desire of the congregation, for a vested choir, and that has grown and improved steadily until it has come to add not only good music, but a quiet dignity to the work of Almighty God in this little country church.

Then we have as fruits of lay co-operation, among others—I may not remember them all, forgive me if I leave out any—the Girls' Friendly Society. I do not believe very many of the congregation understand what a value that is to a Christian congregation, the training up and making friends with and the looking after all the interests temporal and spiritual, of the girls who compose it. I venture to say that wherever that society exists it saves many a girl from going to the devil. It is so here, and the devotion of those who conduct it is beyond any words of praise of mine. They have, during the winter, a period of work for others. They have, during the summer, a period of jollity for themselves, and ought to have it. It gives them pleasure, and pleasure that is overlooked and kept clean and pure. Then the Altar Society, the Boys' Friendly and the Women's Auxiliary, the Men's Auxiliary, the Junior Auxiliary, the boys' and girls' Bible classes, Sunday-school for younger children, the Women's Friendly, the Church Embroidery Society, which works for decent ornamentation of other churches as well as for this church (altar ornamentation, I mean) ; and in the parish building an exercise room for boys and girls in daily and nightly use during fall, winter and spring; in short, a centre of happiness, mental, moral and physical, under wholesome church supervision.

So much for the past and present. What of the future? There is just one thing I want to speak of in this connection, and that is the enlargement of this church building. At the present time there are I do not know how many applications for seats that cannot be granted. There is no room. If Chestnut Hill continues to grow as it has been growing for some time past, and if most of the people who come within easy distance of the church belong to our Protestant Episcopal Church come here, and the number will go on constantly increasing, either one of two things has to happen, either this church must be made larger or we will have two parishes here. I think, and I believe all the business men in the parish will agree with me, that it is better to have one large, strong church congregation than to have two comparatively weak ones. And then, where are you going to put the other? It may be a little further off, in some of the places not yet built up, and be for the use of the people there; but even so, there would be difficulties in the way, because it would be intruding upon the domain of another parish, and our church is very particular about that sort of thing. In order to build a new church anywhere, to set up a new parish anywhere, it is necessary to get the consent of the three nearest rectors, and rectors sometimes have a little objection to bringing other churches too near them. They think that it would take off their own congregations and weaken them, but it can scarcely go anywhere on this side, except between here and St. Martin's. Of course it will not do that; or on the other side of Stenton Avenue, near Grace Church, Mount Airy. But still, where there is a will there is a way, and if people cannot find room to come to a church that is already organized, they will get one somewhere, and somewhere in the neighborhood, so as not to make it too far off for them to go. That is the problem that faces this congregation today. What shall we do? We have plans; the vestry has forseen this for some time, and they had plans drawn by a very competent architect for the systematic enlargement of this particular building. I say systematic. The fully completed plan would be impossible now. It would cost a great deal of money, but it was thought that if we could get enough room to give one hundred and eight new seats (not pews), one hundred and eight single seats, by removing the chancel back, that it would be a very great help, and that it probably would be enough for this generation; because building is very much more expensive now than when this church was built. This church building as it was first put up (I do not now include the changes of the ceiling, which are very great, and the new chancel, but the church as it came from the hands of the builder, able to seat just as many people as it does today) only cost $6,500, which really sounds almost incredible. You could not build it now for four or five times that amount.

As regards the future of this church building, I leave it in your hands. I think it would be a pity both to turn away people because there is no room for them, and to have another parish started very close to this, or to the other two that are here already. It is for you to say what you wish done. I know the feeling about this church building, and I have it myself. I cannot look anywhere here without being *reminded*. But all those objects that are for the memory can be still kept, and in places corresponding to where they now are. And after all, the body of the church itself would not be changed. The change would be in that direction where there fortunately is room enough for quite an enlargement. The second part of the plan added pews with a still larger increase of space, which probably may be left for the next generation, and the final completion will make one of the finest churches anywhere in the Diocese of Pennsylvania. But if we never begin, we never get anywhere, and I leave this matter for your careful consideration, and I trust co-operation.

So much for the very brief sketch. I have been talking longer than I meant to, but I could say no less. The sketch is imperfect, but it may give you some idea of how this parish has grown up to the present time. In conclusion, I want to say two or three words more to this congregation: I cannot find words to express the deep thankfulness that has taken me by storm at your invariable kindness to me. Some people say it is a great thing to be a rector fifty years. I suppose it is, if you keep well all that time, but it has been only by the kindness, the courtesy, the consideration, the love, the bearing by the congregation with steady composure many failings, many faults. I cannot find words to express what I feel. Thank you, God bless and keep you, and when the time comes, as for me it must come before many years, may we all meet before the Throne!

# THE PARISH OF ST. PAUL'S,

## Chestnut Hill,

### From its Organization to June, 1913.

#### Rectors.

Rev. Alexander Shiras, elected November 5, 1855; resigned July 15, 1860.
Rev. William Hobart Hare, elected March 25, 1861; resigned December 15, 1863.
Rev. John Andrews Harris, elected January 26, 1864.

#### Curates.

Rev. J. Clayton Mitchell............July 1, 1892, to November 30, 1897.
Rev. Robert Benedict..............July 1, 1900, to September 1, 1901.
Rev. J. Ogle Warfield..............November 1, 1901, to date.

#### Rector's Wardens.

Cephas G. Childs...................June 18, 1855, to April 16, 1863.
Charles Platt ......................June 23, 1863, to April 13, 1868.
M. Russell Thayer..................April 13, 1868, to April 3, 1880.
Edward S. Buckley.................April 3, 1880, to November 5, 1910.
Edward S. Buckley, Jr..............November 22, 1910, to date.

#### Accounting Wardens.

Frederick Fairthorne ..............June 18, 1855, to October 24, 1857.
Thomas Earp, Jr....................October 24, 1857, to June 30, 1864.
Benoni Lockwood ..................June 30, 1864, to April 17, 1866.
William Henryy Trotter...........April 17, 1866, to November 11, 1868.
Franklin H. Bowen.................November 11, 1868, to April 23, 1870.
Richard Norris ....................April 23, 1870, to June 3, 1874.
Richard C. McMurtrie .............June 22, 1874, to April 19, 1884.
John C. Sims, Jr...................April 19, 1884, to July 8, 1893.
Alexander C. Humphreys...........April 8, 1893, to July 13, 1894.
John C. Sims, Jr...................July 13, 1894, to June 30, 1900.
Isaac Starr .......................June 30, 1900, to date.

#### Secretaries.

Thomas Earp, Jr. .................October 24, 1857, to June 30, 1864.
Benoni Lockwood ..................June 30, 1864, to April 17, 1866.
William H. Trotter................April 17, 1866, to November 11, 1868.
Franklin H. Bowen.................November 11, 1868, to June 4, 1881.
John C. Sims, Jr...................June 4, 1881, to July 8, 1893.
Alexander C. Humphreys...........July 8, 1893, to July 13, 1894.
John C. Sims, Jr..................July 13, 1894, to June 30, 1900.
Isaac Starr .......................June 30, 1900, to date.

43

## VESTRYMEN.

| | |
|---|---|
| John Bohlen | June 18, 1855, to April 29, 1874. |
| Cephas G. Childs | June 18, 1855, to April 16, 1863. |
| Charles Platt | June 18, 1855, to April 1, 1868. |
| Joseph H. Hildeburn | June 18, 1855, to April 19, 1859. |
| Charles Taylor | June 18, 1855, to April 19, 1859. |
| Thomas Earp, Jr. | June 18, 1855, to May 31, 1863. |
| Frederick Fairthorne | June 18, 1855, to May 31, 1861. |
| Clayton T. Platt | June 18, 1855, to May 31, 1861. |
| John C. Bullitt | June 18, 1855, to April 19, 1859. |
| William Henry Trotter | June 18, 1855, to April 3, 1880. |
| Thomas Mason | June 18, 1855, to April 19, 1859. |
| Richard C. McMurtrie | April 19, 1859, to October 2, 1894. |
| William C. Mackie | May 31, 1861, to March 27, 1905. |
| M. Russell Thayer | May 31, 1861, to March 29, 1880. |
| Benoni Lockwood (and Secretary) | June 4, 1864, to April 17, 1866. |
| John P. Brock | September 24, 1865, to Feb. 6, 1869. |
| Richard Norris | April 22, 1867, to June 3, 1874. |
| Franklin H. Bowen | April 13, 1868, to April 10, 1882. |
| Henry Wharton | March 29, 1869, to April 17, 1876. |
| Alexander Biddle | June 3, 1874, to May 2, 1899. |
| Edward S. Buckley | June 10, 1874, to November 15, 1910. |
| Joseph W. Baker | April 17, 1876, to March 29, 1880. |
| Charles B. Dunn | March 29, 1880, to date. |
| C. Stuart Patterson | March 29, 1880, to date. |
| John C. Sims, Jr. | March 29, 1880, to January 6, 1901. |
| George H. North | November 11, 1882, to Dec. 5, 1884. |
| John Whittaker | April 26, 1886, to April 30, 1890. |
| Alexander C. Humphreys | July 27, 1890, to July 14, 1894. |
| William Potter | November 11, 1894, to date. |
| Richard C. Dale | July 14, 1894, to May 22, 1904. |
| Isaac Starr | February 10, 1900, to date. |
| Arthur E. Newbold | January 13, 1901, to date. |
| Radcliffe Cheston, M. D. | May 29, 1904, to date. |
| John H. Craig | April 2, 1905, to date. |
| Edward S. Buckley, Jr. | November 22, 1910, to date. |

### PEWHOLDERS AND SEATHOLDERS.

Abbott, Redman
Allen, Miss Elizabeth O.
Anable, Miss Belle
Anderson, Samuel P. G.
Andrews, Henry W.
Arnott, Wm. W., The Rev.
Asson, William T.
Atwood, William C.

Austin, Samuel H.
Averill, William D.

Bain, Frederick
Baker, Isaac F.
Baker, Joseph W.
Baldwin, Miss Georgiana
Ballard, Ellis Ames

Banks, George A.
Barker, Mrs. George
Barker, S. B.
Barroll, J. Leeds
Barton, J. B.
Belfield, Thomas B.
Bell, Miss Jane E.
Bell, Mrs. J. Bowman
Benson, Edwin N.
Benson, Miss Harriet S.
Benson, Miss Rosalie
Biddle, Alexander
Biddle, Dr. Alexander W.
Biddle, Miss Anne E.
Biddle, Mrs. George
Biddle, George W.
Biddle, James C.
Biddle, Miss Mariamne
Biddle, Louis A.
Biddle, Lynford
Biddle, J. Wilmer
Blake, Mrs. Peter S.
Blanchard, The Misses
Blanchard, William J.
Bohlen, Miss Catharine M.
Bohlen, John
Bohlen, Mrs. John
Bolling, Dr. Robert
Borie, Beauveau
Borie, John J.
Borie, Mrs. J. J.
Boudinot, Mrs. Elias
Bounds, James
Bowen, Edward R.
Bowen, Ezra
Bowen, Franklin H.
Bradford, Willard Hall
Brice, Mrs. Philip H.
Brice, Philip H.
Brock, John Penn.
Brock, Richard Henry
Brown, Miss Ellen R.
Brown, Horace G.
Brown, Thornton
Brown, Edward
Brown, H. P.
Brown, John Wilson, Jr.

Bruce, Mrs. Arthur
Bryarly, Miss Kate Lee
Buckley, Edward S.
Buckley, Edward S., Jr.
Bullitt, John C.
Bullitt, William C.
Burroughs, Joseph H.
Burton, Arthur M.
Burton, Edward
Burton, George W.
Burton, The Misses
Burton, Mrs. Robert
Butcher, Howard
Bartow, Josiah B.
Bohlen, Robert M.
Bartow, Charles B.

Camblos, Pierre
Camblos, Miss
Camm, C. M.
Campbell, Mrs. Dallas Alex.
Campbell, St. George Tucker
Cartwright, Henry R.
Chapman, R. H.
Chase, Reginald H.
Cheston, Dr. Radcliffe
Cheston, Mrs. James
Childs, Col. Cephas G.
Clark, Miss
Clark, Walton
Clark, E. Walter
Clayton, John
Clayton, Mrs. John
Coit, Edward W.
Coit, Howland
Coleman, Mrs. Edward
Coles, Edward
Collins, Alfred M.
Collins, Frederic
Collins, C. W.
Comegys, Walter Douglass
Comegys, Mrs. Walter Douglass
Conway, Mrs. Martha W.
Cooper, Dr. Colin Campbell
Cooper, John Lambert
Cope, Caleb
Cowperthwait, Joseph B.

Craig, J. H.
Crothers, Stevenson
Crothers, William S.
Cowperthwait, Charles T.
Clark, Joseph S.

Dale, Richard C.
Dale, The Misses
Dallett, Elijah
Davis, Edward T.
Davis, Miss C. B.
DeHaven, George B.
Demaray, Mrs. Georgiana
Disston, William
Disston, Jacob S.
Dixon, T. Henry
Dixon, A. J. D.
Dickson, Samuel
Drayton, Miss Harriet D.
Douglas, Edwin V.
DuBois, George T.
Duhring, Rev. H. L., D. D.
Dunmore, Robert S.
Dunn, Charles B.
Dunn, George G.
Durborow, C. B.
Dwight, E. P.
Denkla, Herman A.
Dunn, Edwards S.

Earle, Edgar P.
Earp, Thomas, Jr.
Elkins, William L., Jr.
Emory, Frank
Emory, Miss Ellen
English, Chancellor C.
Eustis, Mrs. A. G.
Evans, The Misses
Ellzey, J. Murray, M. D.

Fallon, John
Fassitt, Miss
Fell, Mrs. Ella G.
Flanagan, James M.
Fletcher, William Meade
Fleming, Mrs. David
Foltz, J. Clinton, M. D.

Forbes, Dr. William
Ford, Mrs.
Fox, S. M.
Freed, Mrs. Rachel
Ford, Bruce
Farnum, Edward S. W.

Gerhard, Miss Louisa
Gibbs, John Willard
Giffin, The Misses
Gilliams, J. J.
Glendenning, R. E.
Goodman, Mrs. S. I. A.
Goodman, William E.
Goodrich, William
Gowen, Francis I.
Graff, Charles H.
Graham, Howard S.
Gratz, Robert H.
Graver, Miss Leonora
Gray, John Gordon
Gray, W.
Griffith, W. O.
Groome, Samuel W.
Groves, A., Jr.
Goodman, Samuel, Jr.
Goodman, Mrs. William E.
Goodman, Mrs. Samuel

Harding, George
Harding, William W.
Harding, William G.
Hare, Mrs. G. Harrison
Hare, Robert Emmot
Harlan, Dr. George C.
Harris, Alan Hale
Harris, George B.
Harrison, Alfred C.
Harrison, Mitchell
Haupt, Gen. Herman L.
Hawley, Warren A.
Hebard, Charles
Heebner, Charles
Heebner, Miss Julia
Heebner, Samuel Y.
Heebner, Philip A.
Heilman, Horace B.

Henry, Morton P.
Hickman, Miss
Hickok, Mrs. Gerardine H.
Hinkle, Daniel S.
Hinkle, G. R.
Hollingshead, Joseph M.
Hollingshead, Mrs. Joseph M.
Hollingsworth, Samuel S.
Hopkin, Mrs. James
Horstman, S. H.
Hovan, Mrs.
Howel, Arch
Hollingsworth, Mrs. S. W.
Hoopes, Mrs. Dawson
Hopkin, C. E.
Hulse, Charles F.
Humphreys, Alexander C.
Hunter, Sarah
Harris, John Andrews, Jr.
Homer, Mrs. Thomas B.
Hillman, John H.

Jackson, Charles M.
Jackson, Francis A.
Jackson, A. A.
Jackson, Mrs. Charles M.
Janney, Spencer M.
Jeans, Mrs. Isaac
Jenks, John Story
Johnson, R. Winder
Johnson, Dr. Russell H.
Johnstone, Mrs. Almyrah
Johnstone, Mrs. A.
Jones, J. H.
Jones, Mrs. J. Cowly
Jones, Miss
Janney, Joseph A., Jr.
Jenks, John S., Jr.
Judson, Oliver Boyce

Keely, Mrs. E. H.
Keim, John O.
Keen, Barton L.
Keim, Mrs. John M.
Kelsey, Albert Warren
Kelsey, Mrs. A. W.
Kemble, Clay

Kent, William C.
Kidder, Walter
Kittson, Lewis
King, Edward S.
Kneedler, Howard S.
Knowles, Rev. Arch. Campbell
Kline, Mrs. Mahlon

Landreth, W. Linton
Landreth, Mrs. Oliver
Lea, Mrs. M. Carey
Lea, Mrs. Charles M.
Levick, Richard
Levick, Mrs. Richard
Lewis, Francis A.
Lewis, Lawrence
Lewis, Miss Mary D.
Lewis, Robert M.
Lewis, Hermann A.
Lewis, William Reed
Littleton, William E.
Lockwood, Benoni
Long, Miss Nancy
Lorenz, William
Lowber, Henry S.

Macauley, The Misses
Machette, E. V.
Mackall, Leonard C.
Mackie, William C.
Markoe, Mrs. John
Martin, Hon. J. Willis
McCall, The Misses
McCouch, H. Gordon
McElroy, Prof. John G. R.
McMurtrie, Richard C.
McMurtrie, The Misses
McNeal, J. Hector
Megargee, Edward
Merritt, Mr.
Mifflin, Miss
Miller, Mrs. John Faber
Miller, Commander Fred'k A.
Mitcheson, McGregor J.
Montgomery, John T.
Moorhead, Mrs. C. F.
Morgan, Randal

Morris, George C.
Morris, The Misses
Morris, Mrs. Stephen
Morris, Mrs. George C.
Morris, Mrs. R. B.
Morris, Henry
Moss, Dr. William
Moyer, Edward E.
Murphy, David M.
Murray, James D.
Mason, John H.
McNaughton, Mrs. Stuart
Muir, John W.
Morgan, Mrs. Reed A.

Naylor, John S.
Neall, Mrs. Frank L.
Neff, Joseph S.
Neiler, Joseph S.
Newhall, Charles A.
Newton, Mrs.
Norris, Henry L.
Norris, J. Parker
Norris, Richard
Norris, John C.
Norris, Mrs. Richard
North, Col. George H.
Newbold, Arthur E.

Ottinger, Mrs. James S.

Page, Edward D.
Page, Joseph F., Jr.
Painter, Mr.
Pancoast, Dr. Dillwyn P.
Patterson, Christopher Stuart
Patterson, Joseph
Patterson, Theodore Cuyler
Peabody, Miss
Penrose, John
Penrose, Walter E.
Penrose, Mrs. J. R.
Pepper, David
Pepper, Dr. George
Pepper, Mrs. William
Pepper, B. F.
Phillips, Alfred Ingersoll

Pidgeon, Theodore F.
Pierson-Hyslop, J. H.
Platt, Charles
Platt, Charles, Jr.
Platt, Clayton T.
Potter, Charles A.
Potter, William
Potter, Mrs. Thomas, Jr.
Powel, Harford Willing Hare
Price, J. Sergeant
Pepper, David, Jr.
Pearson, Mrs. D. Appleton
Platt, Charles, 3d
Pancoast, Henry S.
Pepper, B. Franklin

Ralston, Francis W.
Randall, Miss Susan W.
Reed, Mrs. Henry
Reed, William B.
Register, Mrs.
Remak, Gustavus
Riley, Leonard J., Jr.
Roberts, Jesse
Roberts, Mrs. Jesse
Robins, Thomas
Robinson, Charles A.
Robinson, D. M.
Robinson, Moncure
Rodney, William
Roth, George S.
Rowland, Edward
Rush, Benjamin
Randolph, Mrs. Evan
Rosengarten, Frederic
Reynolds, John Marbury

Scholler, George
Shapleigh, Mahlon S.
Sheppard, Furman
Sharpless, T. W.
Shober, Samuel L.
Sims, John C., Jr.
Sinkler, Charles
Smith, J. Emlen
Smith, Mrs. Joseph P.
Smith, W. Brentwood

Smyth, J. L. N.
Smyth, Mrs. Helen
Smyth, Mrs. Amanda G.
Smucker, J. R.
Snyder, Miss Susan G.
Snyder, W. Frederick
Starr, Theodore
Starr, Isaac
Stephens, J. R.
Stevenson, A. May
Stevenson, Miss Mary
Stewardson, Thomas
Stewart, Thomas MacIntosh
Stewart, William M., Jr.
Stille, Charles J.
Stokes, Charles M.
Stokes, Mrs. Edward
Stone, James N.
Stone, Miss Amy
Strouse, John
Sweeney, Miss Mary
Stokes, Mrs. Thomas P. C.
Snyder, Mrs. William H.
Sexton, William Lord
Steel, A. G. B.
Stewardson, The Misses

Taylor, Charles
Taylor, Mrs. Charles
Taylor, Dr. J. Howard
Thayer, M. Russell
Thayer, Gen. Russell
Thomas, George C.
Thomas, Mrs. George C.
Thorp, Miss Helen
Thouron, Mrs. Augustus
Tilge, Miss Sallie
Torbet, Mrs. Coleman
Toland, Edward D.
Townsend, Mrs. Edward
Trotter, Edward H.
Trotter, Mrs. Edward H.
Trotter, William Henry
Thompson, Mrs. Archibald G.

Van Pelt, Charles E.
Vanuxem, Louis C.
Vaux, Richard
Vaux, The Misses

Wagner, Tobias
Wagner, Mrs. Tobias
Wandell, Dr. James
Watmough, P. G.
Watson, Mrs. Goodwin
Wattson, John B.
Wattson, Thomas C.
Webster, David
Weiser, Mrs. J. F.
Welsh, Edward L.
Welsh, Samuel
Welsh, Mrs. Frank
Wharton, Mrs. Henry
Whittaker, John
Whittaker, Mrs. John
Wilcox, Edmund
Williams, C. N.
Williams, Mrs. Morris
Willing, George
Wiley, Miss
Wilson, Mrs. Seth W.
Wirgman, Mrs. Charles
Wolf, Miss Louise St. C.
Woodward, William H.
Wyatt, Mrs. W. S.
Wagner, Joseph W.
Welsh, John Lowber
Whittaker, Frederic
Whittaker, H. Edward

Yeatman, Mrs. Pope

Zantzinger, Mrs. Alfred
Zantzinger, Ernest
Zebley, John
Zebley, J. Walter
Zantzinger, Clarence C.